BRIDGERTON'S ENGLAND

CONTENTS

INTRODUCTION

It is a truth universally acknowledged that when Netflix invest in a big-budget drama, the results can be truly remarkable. And guided by the skilful hands of Chris Van Dusen and Shonda Rhimes, *Bridgerton* has set a new standard for dramas shot on location. Apart from the beguiling scripts, some inspired casting, a vast wardrobe of 7,500 costumes with a vivid colour palette, there are some jaw-dropping Regency locations to savour. And to these, gentle reader, we will take you.

For the first series of *Bridgerton* over 40 locations were used, dotted around England, from Leigh Court in the south-west to Castle Howard in North Yorkshire and to Chatham Dockyard on the Kent coast. Some of the great stately homes used in the series have been in the same family for years. Wilton House, near Salisbury, is the home of William Herbert, 18th Earl of Pembroke. His ancestor, William Herbert, 1st Earl of Pembroke, was given the estate by Henry VIII over 400 years ago. *Bridgerton* fans will instantly recognise the rear entrance to Wilton as the establishing shot for Simon Basset, Duke of Hastings' London residence, while one peep inside the Double Cube Room will get the heart palpitations going. It is where Queen Charlotte – installed in front of an enormous painting of the 4th Earl Pembroke – and her ladies in waiting viewed the young ladies being presented to court.

And you can visit them both. Almost all of the grand houses, parks and landscape gardens in the series are open to the public at some point in the year; while a few are open all year round. One exception is Lancaster House, a building so opulent it made Queen Victoria envious. In *Bridgerton* it stands in for a variety of rooms in Buckingham Palace and is run by the British Foreign and Commonwealth Development Office. You cannot stroll in with a day ticket to Lancaster House, but you *can* hire it for a wedding. For those nurturing the fantasy of a *Bridgerton*-themed ceremony, there is the opportunity to hire event spaces at virtually every grand location you see on screen.

'We filmed just off the Mall, near Buckingham Palace (Lancaster House). For Hampton Court Palace we were there for an afternoon. It was just amazing. I felt like a Blue Peter winner. I don't think that's something that's ever going to be matched, really. I think that comes from being supported by Netflix. And also Shondaland's massive scope for wanting to put everything they can on screen.'

Jonathan Bailey, Lord Bridgerton

Our small book is the opportunity to indulge in yet another watch of this dramatic gem. Because now you can relive the drama and spot the real-life locations where it was filmed. It will give you a true appreciation of the skill and craft of the film directors, editors and the often unsung heroes, the continuity department and location managers, who have put together this remarkable series.

ROYAL CRESCENT
BATH

The Featheringtons live at No.1 in England's most famous Crescent

Bath's celebrated Crescent was built between 1767 and 1775 by John Wood. His father, John Wood the Elder, had built the nearby Circus, an impressive circular parade of elegant townhouses, but his son went one better with a 500-foot row of 30 terraced houses accompanied by 114 Ionic columns. And when Prince Frederick, Duke of York and Albany, moved into No.1 it became the Royal Crescent.

By modern standards it was an unusual building scheme. Wood designed the neoclassical façade and purchasers bought a certain length of it. They then hired their own architect to design a house to their specification behind the classical frontage – occasionally buyers would buy a double length and so what appeared as two houses was actually one. Take a look round the back of the Royal Crescent and you can see a variety of higgledy-piggledy roof heights and window alignments that came with this approach, a system quaintly referred to as 'Queen Anne fronts and Mary Anne backs'.

Of the crescent's 30 townhouses, 10 are still full-size Georgian townhouses; 18 have been split into apartments and the large central house at number 16 is the Royal Crescent Hotel & Spa. There was outrage in the 1970s when one resident painted their front door yellow instead of the traditional white, but despite the furore planning authorities allowed the change on appeal.

LOCATION ROLES Street scenes, exterior of the Featherington home.

'Knowing it was to be the Featherington's house, we knew they would want to jazz it up a bit to suit the family, so our pale white door was painted a bold blue.'

Amy Frost, Museum Curator
for No.1 Royal Crescent Museum

LEFT
No.30 Royal Crescent is the grand house and private residence bookending the crescent.

ABOVE LEFT
No.1 Royal Crescent is the home to a museum giving an insight into Georgian life above and below stairs.

ABOVE
The deli is situated just off Abbey Green in Bath where the Covent Garden market scenes were filmed. During filming in August and November of 2019 the deli was known as Pickled Greens, but today it is the Abbey Deli.

RIGHT
Bridgerton Location Manager Paul Tomlinson revealed that it took five days of preparation to convert the deli to Modiste. All the serving counters and coffee machines had to be taken out, in August and again in November 2019.

THE ABBEY DELI
2 ABBEY STREET, BATH

The shop of society couturier Genevieve Delacroix has an alternative role as a deli and café, which serves great coffee

In the world of *Bridgerton*, the double-fronted bow windows at 2 Abbey Street belong to the upmarket couture of Modiste. Increased trade with India introduced new materials to Regency London, while revolutionary unrest in France caused an exodus of talented dressmakers from Paris. And so the fashion scene in the capital was vibrant at the beginning of the 19th century, exactly the kind of place for a supposed French expat, Madame Genevieve Delacroix, to set up her business. The *Vogue* of its day, *Le Beau Monde* and its rival, *Literary and Fashionable* magazine, were as essential a read as Lady Whistledown's scandal sheets.

Today, 2 Abbey Street is the location of the Abbey Deli, one of the best-loved delis and cafés in Bath, run by Nicky and Jon Ison. They own two other delis in Widcombe and Larkhall, but the café hasn't always been the occupier of those classic bow-fronted windows. Go back only as far as the 1990s and the shop was the home of Rose Marie Couture (see below). You could almost imagine Lady Featherington and Marina walking out of that door.

LOCATION ROLE Modiste

HOLBURNE
MUSEUM OF ART
GREAT PULTENEY STREET, BATH

Like the Bridgertons' residence, when not hosting society balls, Lady Danbury's home is a prestigious art gallery

Lady Danbury's magnificent home started out in life as the Sydney Hotel, opened in 1799. It was built to accompany the Sydney Gardens, which were a smaller scale version of the Vauxhall Pleasure Gardens, so popular in London at the time. Patrons would enter the gardens through the hotel and could dine in semi-circular rows of supper boxes. Less regular than the Vauxhall entertainments, the gardens held fêtes and soirées, with afternoon tea dances. The hotel lasted until 1836, after which it became a private residence, and then, in 1916, it was purchased to house the extensive art collection of Sir William Holburne.

ABOVE LEFT
In the series Lady Danbury is forever cajoling Simon Basset into social engagements. Indeed, it is at her ball where sparks first fly.

ABOVE
The familiar façade of the Holburne Museum.

RIGHT
A marble sculpture entitled *Diana and Endymion* (1752) by Joseph Plura, displayed in the Brownsword Gallery at the museum. Plura was an Italian sculptor who moved to Bath to open a studio in the 1750s.

Sir William's lifetime of acquisitions included Chinese porcelain, silver, sculpture, Italian bronzes and Old Masters. In 1882 his collection of over 4,000 objects was donated to the City of Bath by his sister, Mary Anne Holburne, and to that the collection has added pictures by English painters Gainsborough, Stubbs and Turner. A radical modern gallery space, a three-story block of glass with ceramic strips, was added at the rear of the building in 2011, perhaps precluding *Bridgerton* filmmakers from ever venturing into Sydney Gardens.

LOCATION ROLE: Lady Danbury's home.

DID YOU KNOW?

Sir William was a naval man, and at 12 years old took part in the Battle of Trafalgar (1805) under Captain Edward Codrington. His ship HMS *Orion* captured the French ship *Intrepide*. You can find his Trafalgar medals on display at the museum.

RANGER'S HOUSE
GREENWICH

The Bridgerton family residence has a strong link to the Regency – it was once occupied by the Duchess of Brunswick

Greenwich was always a popular residence for seafaring men, and what would become known as Ranger's House was built on land next to Greenwich Park around 1723 for Captain (later Vice-Admiral) Francis Hosier.

In 1748 the house came into the possession of the 4th Earl of Chesterfield, a former politician and ambassador who intended to use the house for entertaining; however, after he became deaf in 1752 he withdrew from public life.

It was in 1807 that the house became intertwined with some of the characters we see in *Bridgerton*. George III's sister Augusta, Duchess of Brunswick, took possession of the house and it became known as Brunswick House. She had moved to Greenwich to be close to her daughter Caroline, Princess of Wales, who had been married to the future George IV. Caroline had been given the honorary title of Ranger of Greenwich Park and lived next door in Montagu House (since demolished) where she still entertained royally. Caroline's

ABOVE
The unadorned frontage of Ranger's House, managed by English Heritage and home to The Wernher Collection.

RIGHT
The Bridgerton family pose outside their 'Grosvenor Square' residence, minus Francesca, who is away at boarding school.

FAR RIGHT
For the Netflix series, Ranger's House gained a rose garden and a lot of wisteria blooms.

alternative Regency court and reports of her 'reckless behaviour' did not go down well with other members of the royal family and she was given a financial incentive to leave England in 1814. The Duchess moved out too, making way in 1815 for Princess Sophia Matilda, niece of George III, who was the first Ranger to live in Ranger's House. She was the longest serving resident of Ranger's House, living there until her death in November 1844.

The next Royal in through the door was the third son of Queen Victoria, 12-year-old Prince Arthur of Connaught. He retained the house till the age of 22 and would go on to become a governor of Canada. From 1902 it stopped being a home and became a facility. The London County Council bought the villa in 1902, following lobbying by the local community. It was used as a sports clubhouse and a tea room, and the grounds were converted into a bowling green and tennis courts, which are still there today. When the Council was abolished in 1986 it passed into the hands of English Heritage and is now home to The Wernher Collection of art treasures.

'It was kind of like a really sexy school trip for about nine months. We went around these amazing National Trust sites, and filmed in places that I'd lived near in Greenwich, Rangers House, which was literally a four-minute walk away from where I used to live.'

Jonathan Bailey, Lord Bridgerton

HALTON HOUSE
RAF HALTON

From the outside it may look the wrong era, but Alfred de Rothschild fitted his Victorian mansion with 18th-century interiors

RAF Halton is home to an active military grass airfield where flying has taken place continually since 1913. It is primarily a forces training centre, but within its estate it has Halton House, a Victorian mansion created by Alfred Freiherr de Rothschild in 1880, which, when it's not being lent out to film crews, continues to serve as the Officers' Mess.

More pertinently it serves as the interior of the Bridgertons' London house, and the grand staircase with its gilded ironwork is instantly recognizable. Similar to a character shunned by Lady Whistledown, nobody liked the house when it was built, being variously described as 'a combination of French château and gambling house' and 'a giant wedding cake'. Though it is a product of the late Victorian period, much of the interior harks back to an earlier time, with the dining room and billiard room possessing 18th-century carved wood panelling or *boiserie*.

Rothschild filled it with 18th-century French furniture and Old Masters and held glittering parties, some attended by the Prince of Wales with whom he'd studied Mathematics at Cambridge University. The parties stopped in 1914. The Great War had a terrible impact on its owner

RIGHT
Eloise bellows up the gilded staircase at Halton.

BELOW RIGHT
Halton House was used to portray Edward VIII's French residence in *The Crown*.

BELOW FAR RIGHT
Elizabeth II normally has pride of place on the Halton staircase.

BELOW
The grand entrance hall before the Props Department 'Regencies it all up'.

and after the death of his brothers in 1915 and 1917, Alfred died following a short illness in 1918. The house passed to Lionel Nathan de Rothschild who hated the place and sold it to the RAF, who were already leasing some of the estate land as a training camp.

LOCATION ROLES Bridgertons' grand hall, staircase, smoking room.

WILTON HOUSE
SALISBURY

The estate of the 18th Earl Pembroke provides the exterior for Simon Basset's London residence

Wilton House is an imposing English country house near the village of Wilton outside Salisbury in Wiltshire. It has been the country seat of the Earls of Pembroke for over 400 years after Henry VIII rewarded one of his army officers, William Herbert, by handing him the estate of a former nunnery. Although a small section of the house built for the 1st Earl Pembroke remains, a ruinous fire in 1647 demanded an extensive

rebuilding of the property, at which point illustrious English architect Inigo Jones stepped in. Jones, along with his niece's husband, John Webb, set about designing some of the great state rooms of the house.

The architect was in great demand in the 18th century. Queen Henrietta Maria (wife of Charles I) was a frequent guest at Wilton, and was surprised to find Jones working

ABOVE
The entrance to the Duke of Hastings' London residence.

RIGHT
The Duke plans his day in London over breakfast. Perhaps a little light boxing.

there. At the time of her visit he was
supposed to be finishing the Queen's
House at Greenwich.

Wilton has seven state rooms, which
were the grand show rooms of the
house, designed to impress, should a
monarch or their wife drop round.
State rooms were used exclusively for
elite guests and were typically named,
both as a means of conferring status,
and also so that servants should
know to which room they should
take the champagne. At Wilton, the
star of the show is the Double Cube
Room – designed by Jones and Webb
– which was used by *Bridgerton* for
the nerve-racking presentation of the
débutantes to Queen Charlotte at St
James's Palace.

THE DOUBLE CUBE ROOM

The great room of the house is 60ft
(18m) long, 30ft (9m) wide and 30ft
(9m) high and was built around 1653.
The pine walls have been painted
white and illustrated with foliage
and fruit in gold leaf. Between the
windows (as seen on our Contents
page) are mirrors by Chippendale and
there are console tables by William
Kent.

The grand painting behind the Queen is of Philip Herbert, 4th Earl of Pembroke, with his family, painted around 1635 by Anthony van Dyck. The 4th Earl fell out of favour with King Charles I before the outbreak of the English Civil War.

The other state rooms are the Great Anteroom, the Colonnade Room, the

ABOVE
The eagle eye of Queen Charlotte is upon you, backed up by a portrait of the 4th Earl Pembroke and some fearsome Pomeranians.

LEFT
Looking in through the doors of the Double Cube Room.

Corner Room, the Little Ante Room and the Hunting Room, which is part of the Herberts' private residence. Visitors to Wilton today can see two-thirds of the house; the remaining third is occupied by the current, 18th Earl Pembroke, William Herbert.

PALLADIAN BRIDGE

Prolific Venetian architect Andrea Palladio was influenced by the architecture of ancient Greece, and Palladian architecture reached the height of its popularity in England during the 18th century. Running through Wilton's grounds is the River Nadder, and the 9th Earl Pembroke, working with architect Roger Morris, decided to design a Palladian-inspired bridge to cross it. Ironically, their bridge was based on a design Palladio had worked up for the Rialto Bridge on the Grand Canal in Venice – and rejected. However, the Wilton bridge, which was completed in 1737, was much admired; so much so, that copies were erected at Stowe House, Prior Park (Bath) and Hagley Hall (Worcestershire).

LOCATION ROLES Exterior Duke of Hastings' London home, entrance hall, portrait hall, St James's Palace, Hyde Park.

ABOVE
Take a stroll around Stowe Landscape Garden and you will see an exact copy of Wilton's bridge across the River Nadder.

TOP
Lord Bridgerton, actor Jonathan Bailey, on one of his many rides around the park.

HAMPTON COURT
HAMPTON, MIDDLESEX

Daphne's first great test is to be presented to the court of Queen Charlotte

It is not long before we encounter our first royal palace in *Bridgerton*. After setting out from Grosvenor Square in Episode One, Daphne's carriage passes Buckingham Palace and pulls into a courtyard at St James's Palace. In reality, it is the Clock Court of Hampton Court Palace near Kingston upon Thames. The Clock Court is the second courtyard located beyond the first, Base Court.

The building was planned by Thomas Wolsey, Archbishop of York and his lavish property was completed around 1525, with the best state apartments built around the Clock Court. Henry VIII was soon invited to stay, and very much admired his chief minister's new palace.

Wolsey only got to enjoy his palace for two years. With political enemies circling in the Tudor court the Archbishop thought it wise to gift the palace to Henry VIII in 1528. Though we don't see all of it on film, Daphne's carriage pulls in through Anne Boleyn's Gate, which is adorned with an ancient astrological clock. Boleyn was Henry's second wife, and work was still underway on her apartment in the gatehouse when she was beheaded for adultery in 1536. Her greatest legacy to England was her daughter – the future Elizabeth I.

ABOVE LEFT
Daphne sets off for the palace in Episode One.

ABOVE
Still functioning, the clock shows the time of day, phases of the moon, the month, the date, and most importantly, high water at London Bridge. The main route to the palace was by the Thames in the royal barge and the river was tidal up to nearby Kingston. So Henry's boatmen needed to be sure they wouldn't go aground. He was not a man renowned for his patience.

RIGHT
The Great Vine that George III planted is still going strong.

DID YOU KNOW?

George II was the last monarch to reside at Hampton Court. Once George III took the throne he refused to set foot inside the place, as it reminded him of an incident there when his grandfather struck him.

HATFIELD HOUSE
HATFIELD, HERTFORDSHIRE

*Lady Trowbridge's ball was the scene of
some scandalous goings on*

In the *Bridgerton* location portfolio only Hampton Court has more accompanying history. Hatfield House was once the site of Hatfield Palace where Elizabeth I spent her childhood. Her brother Edward succeeded Henry VIII, but when he died at age 15, it was Elizabeth's older half-sister, Mary, who took the throne. Mary saw Elizabeth as a threat and after a short period of imprisonment in the Tower of London kept her under house arrest at Hatfield. And so it was that in 1558 Elizabeth was sitting under an oak tree in Hatfield Park when she learnt that her sister had died and she was queen.

In 1607 King James I swapped the palace for the home of Robert Cecil, 1st Earl Salisbury, and the Cecil family have been there ever since. Cecil demolished three of the four wings of the palace and used the bricks to build Hatfield House in 1609. The Banqueting Hall still stands, with most of its original roof timbers. Many of them carry the marks of gunshot, from a time when the hall was used as stables, and estate staff took potshots at sparrows.

Hatfield House, with many interiors unchanged since Jacobean times, is a popular filming location for early period dramas including *The Favourite*, the Oscar-winning drama starring Olivia Coleman as a grumpy Queen Anne. Actress Nicola Coughlan (Penelope Featherington)

was particularly excited at acting in the same space as Coleman. Apart from the home and garden of Lady Trowbridge, Hatfield House was also used for some Featherington house interiors and the Library of White's Club where Lord Featherington is regularly pursued for his gambling debts. Sadly, the maze into which Daphne runs after tearing off her diamond necklace, is not accessible to the public.

LOCATION ROLES Lady Trowbridge's house and garden, Featherington interiors, White's Club library, young Simon's schoolroom.

OPPOSITE
The props team replaced the furniture to turn Hatfield's Library into White's.

LEFT
The entrance used for Lady Trowbridge's ball, though minus the caged acrobats.

BELOW
The remaining building from the original Hatfield Palace where Elizabeth I spent her childhood and was later detained.

BELOW LEFT
The outside of the Maze.

STOWE LANDSCAPE GARDEN
STOWE, BUCKINGHAM

Once owned by the richest family in England, Stowe's classic landscape was used to recreate Vauxhall Pleasure Gardens.

VAUXHALL GARDENS

The climax to the opening episode of *Bridgerton* is set in London's famous Vauxhall Pleasure Gardens. It had been the place for reverie since the 1660s; Samuel Pepys recorded a visit at a time when the easiest way to get there was by boat along the River Thames. Previously known as New Spring Gardens, by the 19th century there were concerts, balloon ascents, a Turkish Tent, nightly fireworks and fine dining in between the colonnades of the Temple of Comus.

The fireworks weren't confined to the explosive variety – with five acres of gardens, there was the opportunity for romantic walks away from society's prying eyes. With the rest of the gardens illuminated by thousands of lamps, the unlighted 'dark' or 'close' walks were known as a place for amorous adventures. Thomas Brown in *Works Serious and Comical in Prose and Verse* (1760) described it thus: 'The ladies that have an inclination to be private, take delight in the close walks of Spring-Gardens, where both sexes meet, and mutually serve one another as guides to lose their way; and the windings and turnings in the little wildernesses are so intricate, that the most experienced mothers have often lost themselves in looking for their daughters.'

ABOVE
The Temple of Venus is one of many garden follies at Stowe, where you can take a stroll down three defined paths: The Path of Vice, The Path of Virtue and the Path of Liberty.

RIGHT
Daphne and Simon take to the dance floor at Vauxhall Pleasure Gardens after making their secret compact.

STOWE HOUSE

Stowe has remained very much the same since 1779 when the estate was under the stewardship of Richard Grenville-Temple, the 2nd Earl Temple. The family racked up considerable debts over the years, despite the practice of sons seeking out heiresses to marry to keep the finances flowing. Like all large country houses in Britain, the absence of estate workers, away fighting in the Great War, accelerated the decline of the building. Facing the prospect of demolition, the house was only saved in 1922 by its conversion to a public school. Today, house and garden are run separately – the National Trust operate the extensive landscape park and gardens.

Thomas Kent was responsible for creating many of Stowe's most noted garden features between 1730 and 1738. His first projects were the Temple of Venus, the Goddess of Love, and the Hermitage, which completed the Western Garden in 1731. The Temple looks out across the eleven-acre lake and holds busts of historically licentious characters. Italian muralist Francesco Sleter adorned the walls with lustful scenes, which have sadly disappeared over the years. It was the perfect backdrop to recreate the noise and spectacle of Vauxhall Gardens

THE REFORM CLUB
PALL MALL, LONDON

Lord Bridgerton's gentleman's club, White's, is a London club which once counted fellow cigar-smoker Winston Churchill as a member

The Reform Club was formed in 1836 as a gentlemen's club for both Whigs and Radicals, the two big political parties in Britain at the time, who were committed to political reform. They each had their own exclusive clubs and so an address in Pall Mall was found where they could meet up and discuss change. Charles Barry won the competition to design a new clubhouse by filching ideas from the Palazzo Farnese in Rome. His building in the Italian Renaissance style was ready by 1841 and declared a masterpiece.

Over time the political role of the club has disappeared and today it is a social club with an emphasis on fine dining. True to its pioneering record it was the first gentlemen's club in London to admit women on equal terms, though it *was* in 1981, when Margaret Thatcher was prime minister. There have been many famous members over the years, including H. G. Wells, Winston Churchill, David Attenborough and Dame Kiri Te Kanawa. Novelist

Jules Verne set the beginning of his novel *Around The World in 80 Days* in the Reform Club, where Phileas Fogg has the idea for his grand bet and (plot spoiler coming up) returns there 80 days later. *Monty Python*'s Michael Palin tried to gain entry after repeating the feat via land and sea for his television programme of the same name, in 1989, only to be rebuffed by the dress code police.

OPPOSITE AND BELOW LEFT
Two views of the much-admired Reform Club.

BELOW
Lord Bridgerton and the Duke making plans for Nigel.

BOTTOM
Nigel Berbrooke catches up on the latest Whistledown.

LEIGH COURT
BRISTOL

Leigh Court's Grand Hall played host to the Prince's Ball, where Daphne Bridgerton makes a memorable entrance

The original Leigh Court was an Elizabethan mansion known as Abbots Leigh and played a significant part in British history. After his defeat at the Battle of Worcester in 1651, Charles II spent three nights there with his travelling companion Jane Lane, during his escape to France. The king arrived 'incognito' and his identity was only revealed after he had fled into exile. Once restored to the throne in 1660 he made his unwitting host, George Norton, a knight.

A lack of heirs in the Norton and subsequently the Trenchard family led to the estate falling into disrepair,

and it was in this condition that it was sold to Philip John Miles, a Bristol businessman, in 1811. Miles represents a less glorious part of British history; profiting from enslaved workers and sugar plantations in the Caribbean. He demolished the old building in 1811 and built its successor, a Palladian-style mansion in Bath stone, a quarter of a mile away. As in all country houses of the day, the statement room was the Grand Hall, with its twin staircases, and glass dome high above.

The Miles family continued to occupy the house until 1917, but like all grand country estates, the Great War

put a strain on its finances and it was put up for auction. From then it was used for institutional care, and taken on by the newly formed NHS in 1948. It was sold to private developers in 1988 and has since been restored as a vibrant business hub with extensive conference facilities and rooms to hire for big events. Brides wishing to make Daphne Bridgerton's sumptuous entrance can be assured that Leigh Court is available for weddings.

LOCATION ROLES Prince's Ballroom, Crawford Ballroom.

ABOVE LEFT
The site of Daphne's grand entrance.

LEFT
A smitten Prince Friedrich presents Daphne with a necklace after the Prince's Ball.

ABOVE
That signature double staircase at Leigh Court.

PAINSHILL PARK
COBHAM, SURREY

Simon and Daphne set society tongues wagging when they promenaded in this beautiful 18th-century landscape park

When Simon and Daphne take a turn round the lake in Episode Three of *Bridgerton* they are following in the footsteps of two future U.S. presidents. Painshill Park was used to represent Primrose Hill in London and is one of the finest remaining 18th-century English landscape parks complete with faux ruins and temples. It was created between 1738 and 1773 by Charles Hamilton, although the accompanying house has long since been demolished.

In the Regency period, houses and gardens were open to respectable visitors, who were shown round by the housekeeper and the head gardener for a tip. And so it was that John Adams and Thomas Jefferson

ABOVE
Like Vauxhall Gardens, restored Painshill has a Turkish tent, along with a Crystal Grotto, Ruined Abbey and Gothic Temple.

ABOVE RIGHT
Painshill is one Hamilton project that Thomas Jefferson could approve of.

visited Painshill, Stowe and other country estates in their April 1786 tour of England. Adams wrote: 'Stowe, Hagley (Hall), and Blenheim (Palace), are superb; Woburn, Caversham, and the Leasowes are beautiful. Wotton is both great and elegant, though neglected.' However, he thought that temples and grottoes would look out of place in the more rugged American countryside.

After a succession of private owners the park was finally acquired by Elmbridge Council in 1980. The original features of the landscape garden had declined over the years, but because of its place in history there were many 19th-century engravings and illustrations that could help guide the restoration to Charles Hamilton's original vision. These days it is unnecessary to tip the head gardener – that's all handled by the ticket office.

LOCATION ROLES Primrose Hill, Botanical Gardens.

LANCASTER HOUSE
STABLE YARD, ST JAMES, LONDON

When it was built, it was regarded as the most valuable London residence. Even Queen Victoria was envious …

ABOVE
Victoria was not amused by the size of her neighbour's Grand Hall.

OPPOSITE
Scenes set in Lancaster House's Music Room. Director Tom Verica talks to actors Ruth Gemmell and Golda Rosheuvel while the Pomeranian wrangler steps in to keep the Poms happy. In the background, Brimsley and Mrs Wilson natter on regardless.

Lancaster House is used to portray its London neighbour, St James's Palace, home of Queen Charlotte. It was built for the Duke of York, the second son of George III, using traditional, mellow Bath stone. The Duke died in 1827 before it was finished and the neoclassical house was completed by the 2nd Marquess of Stafford and became known as Stafford House. It was the most valuable private house in London, with a magnificent sweeping staircase and Grand Hall. When Queen Victoria made the short trip down the Mall to visit she remarked: 'I have come from my house to your palace.'

In 1912 industrialist Sir William Lever – founder of the Unilever business – bought the house and renamed it after his home county town, Lancaster. A year later he gave it to the nation. For many years it was home to the London Museum, but after World War II the massive building was taken over by the Foreign and Commonwealth Office, which still operates it today. As a consequence it hosts many international conferences

ID YOU KNOW?

ne British government
ine cellar has resided
in Lancaster House
since 1922.

and meetings, including the G7
summits in 1984 and 1991.

With its wealth of period features
it has deputised for Buckingham
Palace in *The King's Speech* and *The
Crown*, and Lady Rose was presented
to the King and Queen before the
1923 London Season in *Downton
Abbey*, just as Daphne Bridgerton was
presented to Queen Charlotte.

LOCATION ROLES St James's Palace,
Buckingham Palace, concert hall
exterior.

THE QUEEN'S HOUSE
GREENWICH

Prince Friedrich was one of many keen to see a new art exhibition at Somerset House

When the whole of London descends on Somerset House to view paintings in a new gallery in Episode Three, they are indeed visiting a grand house set by the River Thames. The location used in *Bridgerton* is the Queen's House in Greenwich, a little further from the river than Somerset House, but both are buildings in the Classical style. It was commissioned in 1616 by King James I for his wife, Anne of Denmark, supposedly as a gift after an altercation on a hunting trip. Architect Inigo Jones threw aside typical Tudor styles and drafted plans

for what would be England's first classical building. Anne died in 1619 with only the first floor completed and building work only recommenced in 1629 when James's son, Charles I, gave it to his wife Henrietta Maria.

Finally completed in 1636, there was little time to enjoy her extraordinary new home. At the onset of the Civil War in 1642 she was forced into exile, Charles I was executed, and the property seized by the state. After the Restoration of the monarchy in 1660 she returned with her son, Charles II,

ABOVE
The Queen's House was a revolutionary design for its time.

ABOVE RIGHT
The walkways linking the Queen's House depict the streets of Mayfair, a great place to pick up a Whistledown.

RIGHT
The site where a drunken Nigel Berbrooke tries to duke it out with the Duke.

who took the throne. Ironically, instead of going to live in the Queen's House, she was given residence in Somerset House.

The Queen's House was used by members of the royal family until 1805 – the year of Trafalgar – when George III gave the Queen's House to a charity for the orphans of seamen, known as the Royal Naval Asylum. It was taken over by the National Maritime Museum in 1934, who administer it to this day. The Queen's House is famous for its important art collection, including works by artists such as Hogarth, Gainsborough, Reynolds and Turner. A fitting occupation for the former home of Queen Henrietta Maria, a woman born in the Louvre Palace in Paris.

LOCATION ROLES Somerset House exterior, Mayfair street scenes.

ST MARY THE VIRGIN CHURCH
TWICKENHAM

Finally given a licence to marry, the Duke of Hastings and the Bridgerton family attend church in Twickenham

Not far from the River Thames and opposite Eel Pie Island, the church of St Mary the Virgin has an 18th-century interior, but retains its

15th-century medieval tower. The reason for this is simply explained. In April 1713 the nave of the church collapsed. The vicar had anticipated this catastrophic event and moved his congregation outside, preaching sermons in the churchyard and giving thanks that they had been delivered from this perilous event. Many of his parishioners derided the vicar's caution. And then a week later the roof did indeed fall in. It was rebuilt in neoclassical style with some of the older ornaments and monuments being salvaged from the medieval nave. It is still in use as a Church of England place of worship.

ABOVE
The scene of a modest ceremony for Daphne and Simon.

DID YOU KNOW?

Stella McCartney, Yoko Ono, George Martin, Pete Best and Pete Townshend all attended the funeral of Neil 'the fifth Beatle' Aspinall at the church in 2008. Townshend played Bob Dylan's *Mr. Tambourine Man* as a tribute.

DORNEY COURT
WINDSOR

When Daphne and Simon stop off at a coaching inn on their wedding night, they pull up at Dorney Court

England has many magnificent old coaching inns, but the one that the Duke of Hastings books for his wedding night is actually one of England's finest Tudor manor houses and doesn't serve a drop of ale. Located close to the River Thames near Windsor, the house has been in the Palmer family for nearly five hundred years and though there have been Victorian updates to the exterior, the inside is virtually unchanged. In the 17th century Roger Palmer was a firm Royalist and helped campaign to bring Charles II back from exile after the Civil War. With the Restoration of the monarchy in 1660 Charles rewarded Palmer with the Earldom of Castlemaine, then took advantage of his new Earl by seducing his wife, Barbara Villiers. The countess is believed to have had several children by the king. Though you can't stay the night like Daphne and Simon, Dorney Court is available to hire for weddings – the Norman church of St James the Less lies right behind the manor house.

DID YOU KNOW?

Charles II was the first monarch to taste pineapple, after one was brought back from Barbados. Family legend has it that he gave the spiky top to Roger Palmer, who grew it under glass at Dorney Court. There is a 17th-century painting by Hendrick Danckerts of John Rose, the King's Gardener, presenting Charles with a pineapple from this tree. A carved statue of a pineapple stands in the Great Hall at Dorney.

CASTLE HOWARD
YORK

The Duke of Hastings' country estate,
Clyveden Castle, lies 15 miles north of York

Castle Howard in North Yorkshire was commissioned by the 3rd Earl of Carlisle after he had levelled the remains of Henderskelfe Castle in 1699. The earl chose an unusual architect (or surveyor as they were then known), Sir John Vanbrugh, to design his grand mansion.

Vanbrugh was one of Britain's leading playwrights at the time and had never designed a building in his life. Famous for his play *The Provk'd Wife*, which is still performed today, Vanbrugh was assisted by Nicholas Hawksmoor in designing a Baroque masterpiece. In an earlier life, Vanbrugh had been

imprisoned in the Bastille in Paris as a political prisoner, and once released, had spent his days wandering the streets, admiring the French Baroque splendours. After they had drafted the plans for Castle Howard, the pair went on to design the spectacular Blenheim Palace for the Duke of Marlborough.

Sadly Vanbrugh's vision was never fully realised. His ornate West Wing had not been started when he died in 1726 and the 4th Earl ripped up the plans and arranged for his son-in-law to design it in a far simpler, Palladian style. Work on the wing dragged on through the 18th century and it was finally completed in 1811. So today the house has two wings that don't match.

However, it is lucky that both are still standing. In 1940 a fire which started in one of the chimneys ripped through

the building, taking with it rooms in the basement, principal and upper levels, as well as the central cupola, which collapsed into the Great Hall. Girls from Queen Margaret's School in Scarborough, who had been evacuated to Castle Howard, were able to help save precious family heirlooms, but nearly a third of the building was left without a roof. Because the damage had occurred during the early days of World War II, serious restoration did not begin until the 1960s under George and Lady Cecilia Howard.

The dome was rebuilt by 1962, and when the groundbreaking ITV drama *Brideshead Revisited* was filmed there in 1981, the producers helped pay for the reconstruction of the Garden Hall. Restoration work continues to this day, but with a huge estate to maintain it has been a gradual process to bring the Duke of Hastings'

ABOVE
The new Duchess of Hastings is welcomed in through this rebuilt Grand Hall.

ABOVE RIGHT
The rear of Castle Howard.

RIGHT
The Temple of the Four Winds is a delightful place for a picnic, or, a headlong dash in the rain.

country seat back to its full glory.

TEMPLE OF THE FOUR WINDS

When Daphne and Simon race out
of the South Front at Castle Howard
they head in the pouring rain to the
Temple of the Four Winds. This lies at
the eastern end of the Temple Terrace,
with commanding views over the
Northumbrian countryside. It was
also designed by Sir John Vanbrugh
but lay unfinished at the time of his
death in 1726. Like many grand
garden follies it was designed as a
place of contemplation, for reading
and also to take picnics. Beneath its
finely decorated interior there is a
cellar where servants could prepare
food.

LOCATION ROLES Clyveden Castle
exterior and grounds, Clyveden
Grand Hall.

SYON HOUSE
ISLEWORTH, MIDDLESEX

When Queen Charlotte visits King George at Buckingham Palace, she finds him in Syon House's State Dining Room

Syon House was once the home of the familiar-sounding Bridgettines, a medieval order of nuns who built their nunnery, Syon Abbey, here in 1431. Like many of the older houses used in *Bridgerton* it has its fair share of history. A hundred years later, when Henry VIII dissolved the monasteries, it became the property of the crown. His fifth wife, Catherine Howard, was imprisoned for five months at Syon before her execution in 1542 on the grounds of adultery. Five years later, Henry VIII's coffin lay in state, on its journey west from Whitehall to Windsor Castle.

The 1st Duke of Somerset leased the estate from the Crown and had the house rebuilt in the Italian Renaissance style, and then, in 1594, it was acquired through marriage by Henry Percy, 9th Earl of Northumberland, and it has remained in the Percy family ever since.

Before she became Queen Anne, the Princess Anne came to live at Syon with her close friend and confidante Sarah Churchill, the Countess of Marlborough, in 1692. This is the relationship portrayed in the film *The Favourite*, though that drama is set

OPPOSITE
Syon's Great Hall
as created by famed
Scottish architect
Robert Adam. The
Duke of Hastings fills
it with boxes on the
night of his planned
flight abroad.

RIGHT
Queen Charlotte finds
George III dining
alone here, the State
Dining Room of Syon
House.

BOTTOM RIGHT
Queen Charlotte
has to break some
uncomfortable news
to Prince Friedrich in
the Galerie at Syon
House.

in a time after Anne had ascended the
throne. She had been ejected from
her court residence at Whitehall and
Hampton Court by Queen Mary, who
objected to their very close friendship,
but the stubborn princess refused to
dismiss Sarah, even after Mary visited
her at Syon to insist that she did.

One of the bedrooms in Syon
House is known as Princess
Victoria's Bedroom. King William
appointed his friend, the Duchess of
Northumberland, as Victoria's official
governess in 1831, helping her to
prepare for her future role as Queen.
The young princess and her mother
stayed at Syon House many times
over a six-year period and the rooms
remain as they would have been in
Victoria's time, including the original
beds.

LOCATION ROLES Simon Basset's
Great Hall in London, King George
III's dining room Buckingham Palace,
St James's Palace.

CHATHAM DOCKYARD
CHATHAM, KENT

Boxing ring, Georgian garden, Mayfair residence, and slum – the former naval dockyard plays many roles in Bridgerton

No other location works as hard in *Bridgerton* as Chatham Dockyard. Situated to the east of London on the Thames estuary, the naval dockyard had been building and repairing ships from the 16th century. Secretary to the Navy and celebrated diarist Samuel Pepys was a regular visitor, as was Admiral Lord Nelson and Charles Dickens. Today it is the best-preserved dockyard from the age of sail, but ship and submarine building continued here right up until the 1960s. There are many fine Stuart and Georgian buildings on the site, such as the Commissioner's House (1703), the Officers' Terrace (1722) (where Benedict takes his drawing classes

with Sir Henry Granville and more besides), the Guard House (1764), Admirals Offices (1808) and the Cashiers Office where John Dickens, Charles's father, worked from 1817 to 1822. After a brief reprieve to refit ships damaged in the Falklands War of 1982, the dockyard was finally decommissioned in 1984 and is now the home of the Historic Dockyard Chatham.

Apart from the Georgian buildings there is also a wide variety of industrial structures from the Victorian age, and these form the backdrop for Lady Featherington's brazen attempt to shock Marina into accepting an immediate offer of marriage by taking her on a tour of the slums. The Ranger's House in Greenwich, which plays the part of the Bridgertons' family home, has only a rose garden behind it, no trees, and so one of the Georgian gardens in Chatham was needed to hang the two swings that Eloise regularly uses for smoking in the garden.

Simon spends a lot of time sparring with Will Mondrich in a boxing studio, set up in one of the Chatham warehouse buildings, while for the big fight in Episode Eight, the production crew moved to the technological marvel that is Slip No.3. The huge cantilever structure above the shipbuilding slipway was the widest-span timber building in Europe when it was constructed in 1838 and today is the home to a variety of vehicles and exhibits ... and dodgy boxing matches.

LOCATION ROLES Simon's sparring gym, Sir Henry Granville's street, Bridgerton garden, Lady Featherington's slums, Lombard Street printers, Prize Match arena.

PLACES TO VISIT

With the world slowly emerging from Covid restrictions, some of the locations used in the series may alter their pattern of opening, so please check their respective websites before scheduling a visit. If you would like to book a Bridgerton wedding venue, there is ample choice. Only the Queen's House, Greenwich and Halton House don't offer that facility at present.

BATH – ROYAL CRESCENT

Open to the public all year round; however, as it is often used in films, from time to time it will be closed off for short periods – and to the sound of thundering hooves.

BATH – ABBEY DELI

Open seven days a week for coffee, cake and couture. Or at least two of those three.

BATH – HOLBURNE MUSEUM OF ART

Open as a museum all year round, you can also take a peep around the back into Sydney Gardens, a former pleasure garden of modest proportion.
https://www.holburne.org/planning-your-visit/

RANGER'S HOUSE

Located on the boundary of Greenwich Park, today it is home to an art gallery, The Wernher Collection, but no wisteria.
https://www.english-heritage.org.uk/visit/places/rangers-house-the-wernher-collection/prices-and-opening-times/
Also available for weddings, but don't count on there being two swings out the back.

HALTON HOUSE (RAF HALTON)

Serves as a functioning mess hall for officers. The house is opened annually to the public for open days, normally in National Heritage Week in September. It may well be, with the interest generated by the Netflix series, that they put on more in the future.
https://www.heritageopendays.org.uk/news-desk/news/my-heritage-open-days-halton-house

WILTON HOUSE

The House and Grounds are usually open to visitors between May and September. The 18th Earl Pembroke also owns a pub – the Pembroke Arms – you can find links to it on the house website.
https://www.wiltonhouse.co.uk/opening-and-admissions/

HAMPTON COURT PALACE

This UNESCO World Heritage Site is open to the public all year round, with the annual Hampton Court Flower Show in July, summer concerts organised in the Base Court and ice-skating in December and January.
https://www.hrp.org.uk/hampton-court-palace/visit/

HATFIELD HOUSE

The park and gardens are open to the public from April, and Hatfield House is open from June. If you want to see inside the remaining Hatfield Palace building, be sure to contact Hatfield in advance, as it is often closed for private events.
https://www.hatfield-house.co.uk/your-visit/opening-times-prices/

STOWE LANDSCAPE GARDEN

The Landscape Garden (National Trust) is separate from Stowe House (Stowe House Preservation Trust). The Temple of Venus is in the Western Garden and the National Trust gardens and park is open to visitors year-round. https://www.nationaltrust.org.uk/stowe
Available as a wedding venue, the Temple of Venus has guest capacity for 40 inside or outdoors for 500, as long as you are confident about weather forecasting.

THE REFORM CLUB

Each September the club participates in Open House London, when hundreds of buildings in London open their doors. You can't book a solo tour but organised groups of ten or more are welcome on weekday mornings. Those taking part are invited to contribute £15 per person to the Reform Club Conservation Charitable Trust. Visitors are required to adhere to the Club's formal dress code with gents required to wear collar, jacket and a tie is appreciated. No flip flops, trainers or hiking boots. Ladies should be formally dressed, so we advise no hot pants.
https://www.reformclub.com/Home

LEIGH COURT

Available for business conferences, meetings and delegate events. Advertised primarily as a venue available for hire, including weddings. https://www.leighcourt.co.uk/

PAINSHILL PARK

Owned by Elmbridge Borough Council and managed by the Painshill Trust, the Park with its grottoes and follies is open to the public with an entry charge.
https://www.painshill.co.uk/visit-us/

LANCASTER HOUSE

Managed and run by the Foreign, Commonwealth & Development Office. Not open to the public, but available for G7 conferences, private events and venue hire through the FCDO.
https://blogs.fcdo.gov.uk/stories/lancaster-house-a-world-class-venue-for-your-special-event/

THE QUEEN'S HOUSE

The Queen's House is part of the Royal Museums Greenwich, which include the famed tea clipper *Cutty Sark*, the Royal Observatory and the National Maritime Museum. It's normally open all year round to display an 'internationally renowned' collection of art.
https://www.rmg.co.uk/queens-house

ST MARY THE VIRGIN CHURCH

St Mary's is an active Church of England congregation in Twickenham. The cemetery contains the graves of former colonial American governors for Virginia and New York.

DORNEY COURT

The Tudor manor house is open during the summer, and throughout the year by appointment (usually to groups of 20 or more). Don't expect to see the Duchess of Hastings' bedroom upstairs – it's actually a sitting room downstairs. Available for wedding hire.
https://dorneycourt.co.uk/visit/opening-times-prices/

CASTLE HOWARD

The grounds are usually open to the public from March to November, with pre-bookable private group talks and tours also available.
https://www.castlehoward.co.uk/visit-us/visitor-information/group-visits/special-tours-and-talks.
It can 'occasionally' be hired for private events.